Gift of the
Friends of the Library

W9-CNA-348

BASKETBALL

Rennay Craats

Weigl Publishers Inc.

Published by Weigl Publishers Inc.

123 South Broad Street, Box 227

Mankato, MN 56002

USA

Library of Congress Cataloging-in-Publication Data available upon request from the publisher.
Fax (507) 388-2746 for the attention of the Publishing Records Department.

ISBN 1-930954-05-0

Printed in the United States of America

1 2 3 4 5 6 7 8 9   05 04 03 02 01

Project Coordinator

Rennay Craats

Layout and Design

Warren Clark

Copy Editor

Heather Kissock

Photograph credits

Cover: Visuals Unlimited (H.Q. Stevens); Title: Frozen Motion Photography (Bernie Steenbergen); Contents: Reuters/Archive Photos (Tami L. Chappell); Corel Corporation: pages 20L, 20R; EyeWire: page 7R; Frozen Motion Photography: pages 6/7, (Bernie Steenbergen),10R (Bernie Steenbergen), 12L (Bernie Steenbergen), 12R (Bernie Steenbergen),14L (Bernie Steenbergen), 22/23BL (Bernie Steenbergen); Globe Photos Inc: pages 16L (Andrea Renault),18R (Walter Weismann), 19L (John Barrett),19R (Jerry Wachter); Monique de St. Croix: pages 5R, 8, 11R, 13R,15T, 21L, 21R; National Archives of Canada: page 4; RangeFinders/Globe: pages 17L (Mitchell Levy), 17R (Mitchell Levy); Reuters/Archive Photos: pages 5L (Sam Mircovich), 11L (Brent Smith), 13L (Jeff Topping), 14R (Tami L. Chappell),15B (Gary Cameron),16R (Jim Bourg), 18L (Peter Jones), 23R (Mike Blake); Visuals Unlimited: page 10L (H.Q. Stevens).

Contents

What is Basketball?

D r. James Naismith taught university physical education in Springfield, Massachusetts. In the winter, his students did not have many games to play inside. He decided to create a new game. He asked a janitor to hang two peach baskets at either end of the gymnasium. Players bounced a soccer ball down the court and tried to throw it into the peach baskets. Within ten years, the baskets were replaced with metal hoops with nets sewn around the edges. A **backboard** was added so the ball would not land in the crowd after a shot. Finally, the soccer ball was replaced by a larger, leather ball. Teams in the early 1900s played basketball as we know it today.

Dr. Naismith (center) coached many early basketball teams.

Basketball is played by two teams of five. Games often consist of two twenty-minute halves. In professional basketball, there are four twelve-minute quarters.

To win, a team needs to score more points than its opponent. The offensive team is the one with the ball. Its members **dribble** the ball down the court and try to shoot it into the basket. The defensive team tries to stop them from scoring. Baskets from within the **three-point line** are worth two points. Baskets from outside the three-point line are worth three points.

Slam dunks are exciting basketball shots. Fans love to watch their favorite players score points this way.

Three-point shots help keep the winning team ahead of its opponent.

CHECK IT OUT

Read about Dr. James Naismith and the beginnings of basketball at **www.hoophall.com/hoophistory/ naismith.cfm**

5

Getting Ready to Play

Basketball players do not need a lot of equipment. The game does not involve contact, so players do not wear padding.

Basketball players wear loose-fitting shorts. They are comfortable for the players and allow them to move easily.

The most important piece of equipment for basketball players is shoes. The shoes are light so players can run quickly. Shoes with rubber bottoms stop players from slipping on the floor. Shoes also have support for the players' ankles to prevent injuries.

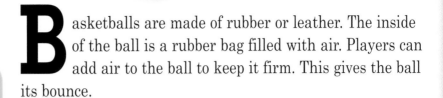

Players wear jerseys with a number on the back. These shirts often do not have sleeves so players can easily shoot or pass the ball. This style of shirt is also cooler for the players.

Basketballs are made of rubber or leather. The inside of the ball is a rubber bag filled with air. Players can add air to the ball to keep it firm. This gives the ball its bounce.

Players shoot the ball at the basket. The metal hoop is almost twice as wide as a basketball. The netting hanging from the basket is often made of nylon rope.

The basket is attached to a backboard. The backboard is made of wood, **fiberglass**, or graphite. Backboards keep the ball from going out of bounds every time it is shot. They also help players shoot. They bounce the ball off the backboard into the net.

National Basketball Association (NBA) backboards are flat and transparent. A small square is often painted on backboards to help players aim their shots.

The Court

Basketball is played on a surface called a court. The 10-foot-high baskets hang at either end of the court. The court has many lines and circles painted on it. The boundaries are shown by the baseline and the sideline. Players cannot step outside of these lines with the ball.

Courts in the NBA are usually 94 feet long and 50 feet wide.

The game begins at the center circle. From there, players run up and down the court to score baskets and try to stop the other team from scoring. The lines on the court tell them where they have to shoot from to get three points. The lines also show them where to line up for **free throws.**

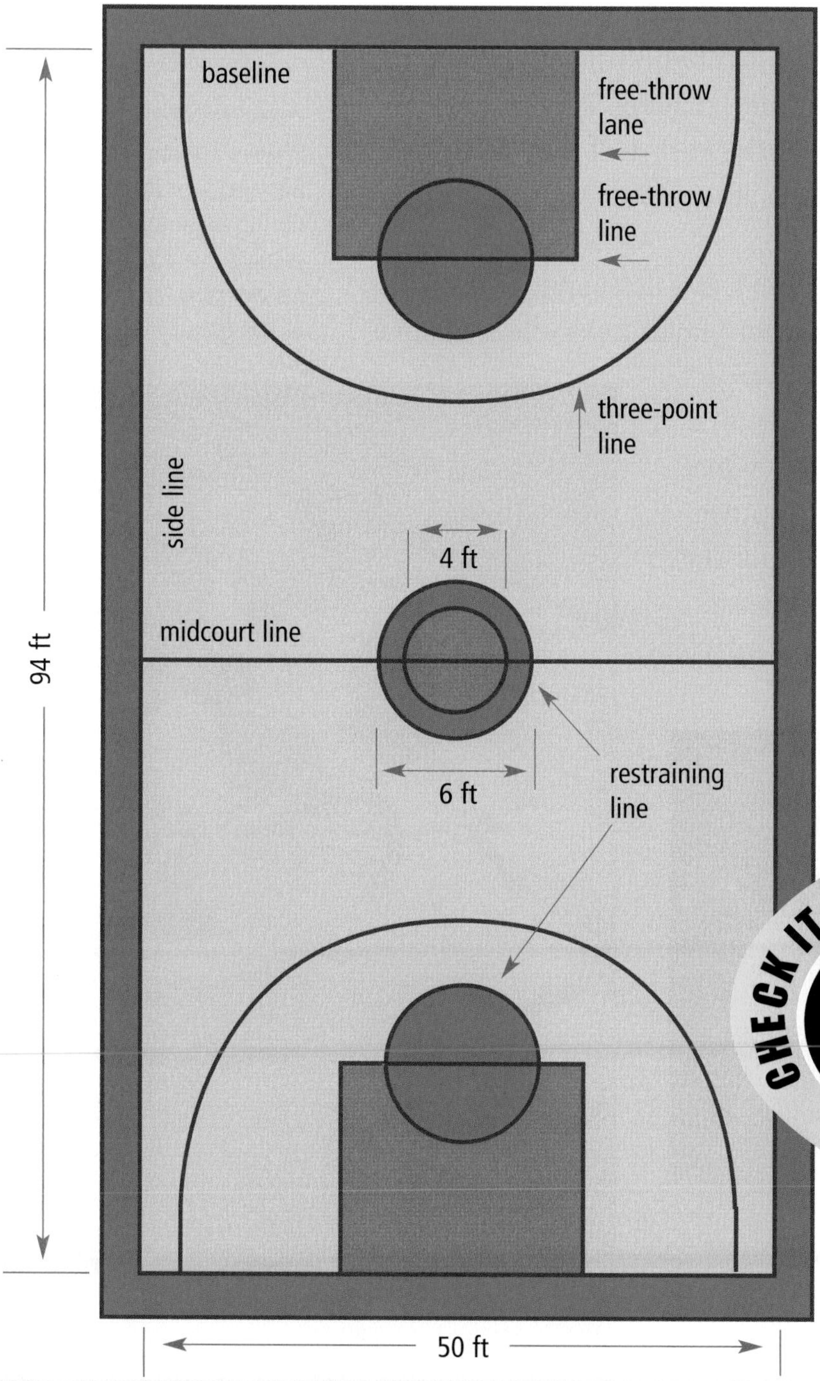

baseline

free-throw lane

free-throw line

three-point line

side line

4 ft

midcourt line

6 ft

restraining line

94 ft

50 ft

CHECK IT OUT

To learn about where professional basketball players play, surf over to

www.findhoops.com/arenas.html

Order on the Court

The player with the ball has to dribble, pass, or shoot. Once the player touches the ball with both hands, he or she cannot continue dribbling. Players have twenty-four seconds to shoot at the basket. If they do not, they have to give the ball to the other team.

Basketball is not a **contact sport**. If a defensive player pushes, bumps, or knocks another player, he or she is given a **foul**. If the foul occurs as a player is shooting at the basket, he or she is given two free throws. If the shot goes in the basket, the player is given two points for the basket plus one foul shot. Foul shots are worth one point each. The other team cannot block or interfere with these penalty shots.

Players are only allowed four fouls during a game. If they receive five fouls, they cannot play for the rest of the game.

Players swarm the net after a shot is made to catch a possible **rebound**. They are not allowed to touch the ball if it is above the basket.

If the foul occurs at any other time, there is a **throw-in**. The member of the fouled team takes the ball out of bounds and throws it in to his or her teammates. A throw-in also occurs when the ball is thrown or knocked out of bounds. The last team to touch the ball before it bounces out of bounds loses **possession**. The other team throws the ball in. Throw-ins are also used after a team scores. The team that was scored upon throws the ball in from the baseline and tries to score at the other end.

The referee and umpire keep order on the court. The referee watches what is happening close to the basket. The umpire watches the other players. If they see players breaking the rules, they blow their whistles to stop the play. The referee makes the final decisions. If players or coaches argue with the referee, they can be thrown out of the game. Referees can also penalize the team for arguing by giving the other team free throws.

Many coaches, including Indiana Pacers coach Larry Bird, are experienced basketball players.

A throw-in is made where the ball bounces out of bounds.

11

Positions

There are three positions on a basketball team. The center is the tallest player on the team. Centers take the **jump ball** at the beginning of the game. The centers from each team meet at the center circle. The referee throws the ball straight up in the air. The centers try to tip the ball to their teammates, who are standing outside the circle. Centers also stay close to the basket to catch rebounds, or missed shots. Being tall helps them reach higher and catch the ball.

A jump ball is also taken if players from opposing teams touch the ball at the same time before it goes out of bounds. The jump ball is then taken at the nearest circle.

Players must work together to defend the net.

Guards control the plays on the court. They are good dribblers and fast on their feet. Point guards usually bring the ball down the court. They then pass it to other players so they can shoot. Shooting guards are good dribblers and good shooters. They can shoot well from anywhere on the court. It is often the guards who shoot three-point shots.

Forwards have to practice shooting close under the basket.

Forwards stay close to the basket. They usually stand on either side of the basket. Small forwards are good shooters. They make many of the shots at the basket. Power forwards are taller. They help the center rebound and make baskets from the bottom of the court.

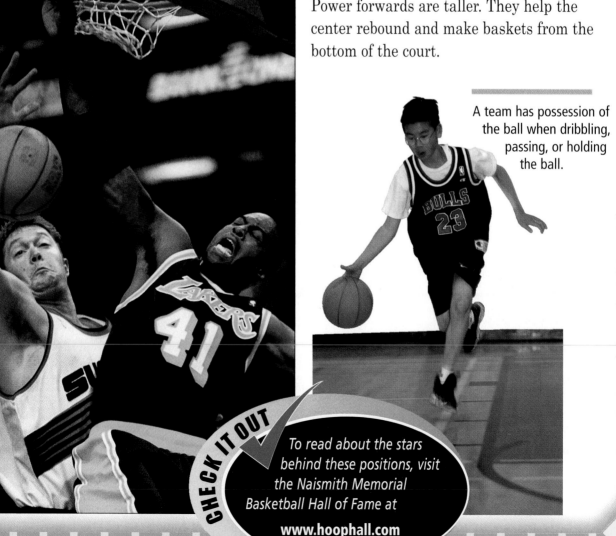

A team has possession of the ball when dribbling, passing, or holding the ball.

CHECK IT OUT

To read about the stars behind these positions, visit the Naismith Memorial Basketball Hall of Fame at **www.hoophall.com**

Making the NBA

Many children grow up playing basketball at their school yards and playgrounds. They often join community or school teams to learn the skills of the game. College and university basketball teams are great places to get experience and get noticed by the National Basketball Association. Players at the college level want to make the final four.

The final four is a college play-off that is watched by millions of people. It is called March Madness. Many players on successful teams in March Madness get **scouted** by professional basketball teams. But not all professional basketball players go to college. Some outstanding players are noticed while they are in junior and senior high. They are scouted at the age of seventeen or eighteen.

As did Grant Hill, many college stars make names for themselves in the NBA.

Cheering on teammates is important at all levels of play.

CHECK IT OUT

Follow your favorite teams at

www.nba.com

Most young basketball players dream of playing in the NBA. Professional basketball players work hard for eighty-two games each season to make the play-offs. The top eight teams in each division play each other. These are called the Conference Championships. The two winning teams play each other for the NBA Championships. The Boston Celtics have won the championships the most times, with sixteen titles.

Practicing with a friend can improve both skill and endurance.

Many NBA stars represented the United States at the 1996 Olympics. The "Dream Team" won the gold medal.

Superstars of the Sport

Basketball has seen many heroes since the NBA was formed in 1949. Many of these players have inspired children to play the game, too.

#23 MICHAEL JORDAN

POSITION:
Guard
TEAM:
Chicago Bulls
SIGNED TO THE MAJORS:
1984

Career Facts:

- In the tenth grade, Michael was cut from the basketball team.
- Michael led the NBA in scoring nine times and was named Most Valuable Player (MVP) five times.
- During his brief retirement starting in 1993, Michael played professional baseball.
- Michael led the Bulls to three NBA championships in a row.
- Many fans, coaches, and critics think Michael was the best player to ever play basketball.

#33 LARRY BIRD

POSITION:
Forward
TEAM:
Boston Celtics
SIGNED TO THE MAJORS:
1979

Career Facts:

- In Larry's last season, 1991-1992, he earned more than $7 million. The average salary in the league was just over $1 million!
- Larry was voted Most Valuable Player three times.
- Few of Larry's coaches in college thought he would make the NBA. He worked at basketball all the time and proved them wrong.
- The year before Larry joined the Celtics, the team had won 29 and lost 53 games. With Larry, the team turned their record around and won 61 and lost only 21.
- In 1985-86, Larry finished in the top ten in five categories including scoring, steals, and free throws. It was one of the greatest seasons ever by any player.

#13 WILT CHAMBERLAIN

POSITION:
Center
TEAM:
Los Angeles Lakers
SIGNED TO THE MAJORS:
1959

Career Facts:

- Wilt was a Harlem Globetrotter.
- In 1962, Wilt had the league's highest points per game average. He scored an average of 50.4 points every time he played.
- Wilt's 1962 record for scoring 100 points in a game has never been beaten.
- At 7 feet 1 inch, Wilt was the NBA's first giant superstar.
- Wilt led the league in rebounds eleven times and was the top scorer seven times in a row.

#6 BILL RUSSELL

POSITION:
Center
TEAM:
Boston Celtics
SIGNED TO THE MAJORS:
1956

Career Facts:

- Bill was 6 feet 10 inches tall.
- In his first year, Bill was the only African-American player on the team.
- With Bill as the center, the Celtics won eleven championships in thirteen years. Eight of these wins were in a row.
- At 32 years old, Bill became the first African American to coach any major professional sports team. He coached his old team, the Boston Celtics.
- Bill was named the best basketball player ever by the Professional Basketball Writers Association of America in 1980.

Superstars of Today

The basketball stars of today are breaking records and amazing fans.

#15 VINCE CARTER

POSITION:
Forward
TEAM:
Toronto Raptors
SIGNED TO THE MAJORS:
1998

Career Facts:
- Vince was the 1998-1999 **Rookie** of the Year.
- Vince led his team in many areas including scoring and blocked shots.
- The NBA named Vince the Player of the Week. He was the first Raptor to ever have this honor.
- Vince wears size sixteen shoes.
- Fans look forward to Vince's incredible slam dunks.

#33 GRANT HILL

POSITION:
Guard
TEAM:
Detroit Pistons
SIGNED TO THE MAJORS:
1994

Career Facts:
- Grant is the first NBA rookie to lead the All-Star voting.
- Academics was important to Grant. He chose Duke University for more than just basketball.
- Grant played in the 1995 All-Star game after playing professional basketball for only three months.
- Grant never wanted to stand out. His coaches told him not to be afraid to be great.

#50 REBECCA LOBO

POSITION:
Center and Forward
TEAM:
New York Liberty
SIGNED TO THE MAJORS:
1997

Career Fact:

- Rebecca is 6 feet 4 inches tall.
- In 1995, Rebecca led her university basketball team to an undefeated season.
- Rebecca was a star of the 1996 Olympic gold medal basketball team.
- Despite battling injuries, Rebecca led her team in areas including rebounds and blocked shots.

#12 JOHN STOCKTON

POSITION:
Guard
TEAM:
Utah Jazz
SIGNED TO THE MAJORS:
1984

Career Facts:

- John played in nine straight All-Star games.
- In 1996, John was chosen as one of the fifty greatest players in NBA history.
- John is the all-time NBA **assists** and steals leader. He holds almost every passing record.
- In 1996, John joined several other professional basketball players on the Dream Team at the Olympic Games. The team won a gold medal.
- In John's more than fifteen years in the NBA, he has not won a championship.

CHECK IT OUT

Find out more about the women's basketball league at

www.wnba.com

Staying Healthy

Basketball is a fast game of running and jumping. To keep up with the rest of the team, basketball players need to stay healthy. A balanced diet of fruit, vegetables, meat, and breads and cereals helps keep their bodies running well. These healthy foods provide important vitamins, minerals, fiber, and proteins that keep players working at their best.

CHECK IT OUT

Learn more about eating healthy by visiting

www.nalusda.gov/fnic

Basketball players need to keep their muscles in shape, too. Stretching is important to prevent injuries. Players should stretch out their shoulders, back, and legs before stepping onto the court. There are also simple ways to strengthen leg muscles. Ski tucks help with strength and jumping.

To train with ski tucks, players stand with their feet together and jump straight in the air. They pull their knees into their chests. Each time they do the drill, they try to jump higher. To further improve their jumping, they stand against a wall and jump up as high as they can. They stretch as far up the wall as possible and try to reach a higher point every day.

Basketball Brain Teasers

Test your knowledge of this fast-paced sport by trying to answer these basketball brain teasers!

Q Are all basketball players very tall?

A No. Some very successful NBA players are quite short. Tyrone (Muggsy) Bogues stands only 5 feet 3 inches, and Spud Webb is only 5 feet 7 inches tall.

Q What happens if players do not dribble?

A A player can only take one and a half steps while holding the ball. Any more than that is called traveling. If a player travels, the play is stopped. The ball is given to the other team.

Q Is the Women's National Basketball Association popular?

A In the first year, more than a million fans went to see WNBA games. The association is adding more teams and making the season longer. It is very popular.

Q What is the record number of points ever scored by a center?

A Los Angeles Lakers center Kareem Abdul Jabbar scored 38,387 regular-season points in his career. He scored another 5,762 points through the play-offs.

Q What is an air ball?

A An air ball is a shot that misses the backboard and does not go in the basket.

Q Who were the tallest basketball players to play in the NBA?

A There have been many very tall players in the NBA. Manute Bol and Gheorge Muresan towered at 7 foot 7 inches.

Glossary

assists: passing the ball to a teammate, who then scores

backboard: the rectangular board to which the basket is attached

contact sport: a sport where physical contact between players, such as tackling and checking, is allowed

dribble: bouncing the ball off the floor with one hand at a time

fiberglass: a material made of very fine strands of glass

foul: a penalty for illegal contact

free throws: shots that a fouled player takes from the foul line—no one can try to block this shot

jump ball: when the referee tosses the ball straight up between two opposing players, and the players try to knock the ball to their teammates

possession: control of the ball by a player or team

rebounds: missed shots that bounce off the backboard or basket

rookie: a player in his or her first year

scouted: being noticed by representatives of higher sports teams

slam dunks: shots where the player jumps above the net and drives the ball into the basket

three-point line: the large half-circle drawn toward the outside of the basket

throw-in: putting the ball back in play from out of bounds

Index